Fishkeeping

Teaching Tips

Turquoise Level 7

This book focuses on the grapheme **/ow/**.

Before Reading

- Discuss the title. Ask readers what they think the book will be about. Have them support their answer.
- Ask readers to sort the words on page 3. Read the sounds and words together. Reinforce that /ow/ can have a long /o/ sound or an /ow/ sound, and is "now."

Read the Book

- Encourage readers to read independently, either aloud or silently to themselves.
- Prompt readers to break down unfamiliar words into units of sound and string the sounds together to form the words. Then, ask them to look for context clues to see if they can figure out what these words mean. Discuss new vocabulary to confirm meaning.
- Urge readers to point out when the focused phonics grapheme appears in the text. Does it have a long /o/ sound or an /ow/ sound?

After Reading

- Ask readers comprehension questions about the book. In what ways are people caring for pet fish in the book?
- Encourage readers to think of other words with the /ow/ grapheme. On a separate sheet of paper, have them write the words into two columns: one under the long /o/ sound and the other under the /ow/ sound.

© 2024 Booklife Publishing
This edition is published by arrangement with Booklife Publishing.

North American adaptations © 2024 Jump!
5357 Penn Avenue South
Minneapolis, MN 55419
www.jumplibrary.com

Library of Congress Cataloging-in-Publication Data is available at www.loc.gov or upon request from the publisher.

ISBN: 979-8-88996-873-3 (hardcover)
ISBN: 979-8-88996-874-0 (paperback)
ISBN: 979-8-88996-875-7 (ebook)

Decodables by Jump! are published by Jump! Library.
All rights reserved. No part of this book may be reproduced in any form without written permission from the publisher.

Photo Credits

Images are courtesy of Shutterstock.com. With thanks to Getty Images, Thinkstock Photo and iStockphoto. Cover – worker. 4–5 – bluecinema, Sergii Figurnyi. 6–7 – New Africa, uventa6. 8–9 – Chaikom, Noheaphotos. 10–11 – Chaikom, mariati. 12–13 – Ju Jae-young, Tretyakov Viktor. 14–15 – Frantisek Czanner, simonlong. 16 – Shutterstock.

Can you sort these words into two groups? One group has **ow** as in **crown**. One group has **ow** as in **slow**.

tower

cow

owl

tow

grow

arrow

snow

Keeping pet fish might not seem difficult, but there is quite a lot to think about when you own fish.

Not all fish have the same needs, so you must make sure that each one is cared for in the correct way.

You might think that fish like being in fishbowls, but this is not true. Fishbowls are often too little and can be bad for fish.

Fish need room to swim around. If you plan to have lots of fish, make sure to keep them in a tank that is not crowded.

One more reason that fishbowls are bad is that they do not allow the right amount of air in.

A tank that has no air pumped into it will get stagnant, which will kill the fish. You need a tube that blows a constant flow of air into the tank for the fish.

Air tube

Fish tanks need to be cleaned often. It will not take long for fish to make a tank dirty.

Having a powered filter is a good start, but you will still need to wipe it clean now and then.

Filter

You can decorate a tank to make it an interesting home for fish. Add gravel down at the bottom of the tank. Get some plants in there too.

Gravel

Some fish like to hide, so structures such as towers and rocks with holes are good to have as well.

It is important that you remember to feed the fish. But only feed them when they need it. Giving fish too much food at once can be bad for them.

When the tank is clean and the fish are fed, all that is left to do is sit back and enjoy the show!

Say the name of each object below. Is the "ow" in each an /ow/ sound or a long /o/ sound?